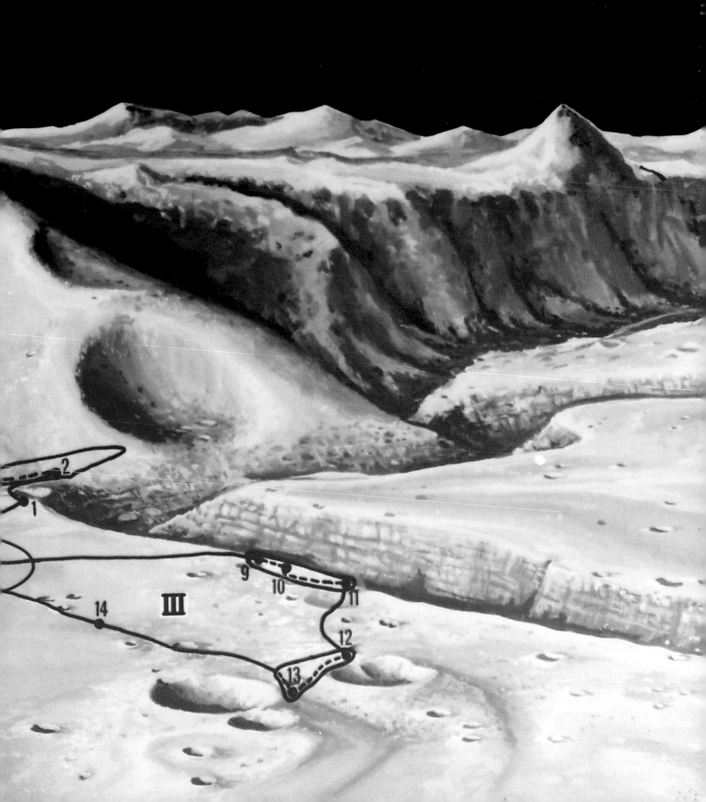

DESTINATION: MOON

BY ASTRONAUT
JAMES IRWIN

To my grandchildren
Joshua and Jessa,
and to all the children of the blue planet.

Cover and interior design by Multnomah Graphics
Designer Bruce DeRoos

DESTINATION: MOON
© 1989 by Multnomah
Portland, Oregon 97266

Multnomah is a ministry of Multnomah School of the Bible, 8435 N.E. Glisan Street, Portland, OR 97220.

Printed in the United States of America

Library of Congress Cataloging-in-Publication Data

Irwin, James B. (James Benson)
    Destination: Moon / James Irwin.
        p. cm.
    Summary: James Irwin describes his training and schooling to become an astronaut and his participation in the Apollo 15 voyage to the moon where he conducted experiments, explored the moon's surface, and made a spiritual discovery.
    ISBN 0-88070-307-5
    1. Space flight to the moon–Juvenile literature. 2. Project Apollo–Juvenile literature. 3. Irwin, James B. (James Benson)–Juvenile literature. [1. Space flight to the moon. 2. Project Apollo. 3. Irwin, James B. (James Benson) 4. Christian life.]
I. Title
TL799.M6I78   1989
629.45'4–dc19   89-3078
                                                                                CIP
                                                                                AC

89   90   91   92   93   94   95   96   97   98   –   10   9   8   7   6   5   4   3   2   1

DESTINATION:
MOON

BY ASTRONAUT
JAMES IRWIN
WITH
AL JANSSEN

MULTNOMAH

Portland, Oregon 97266

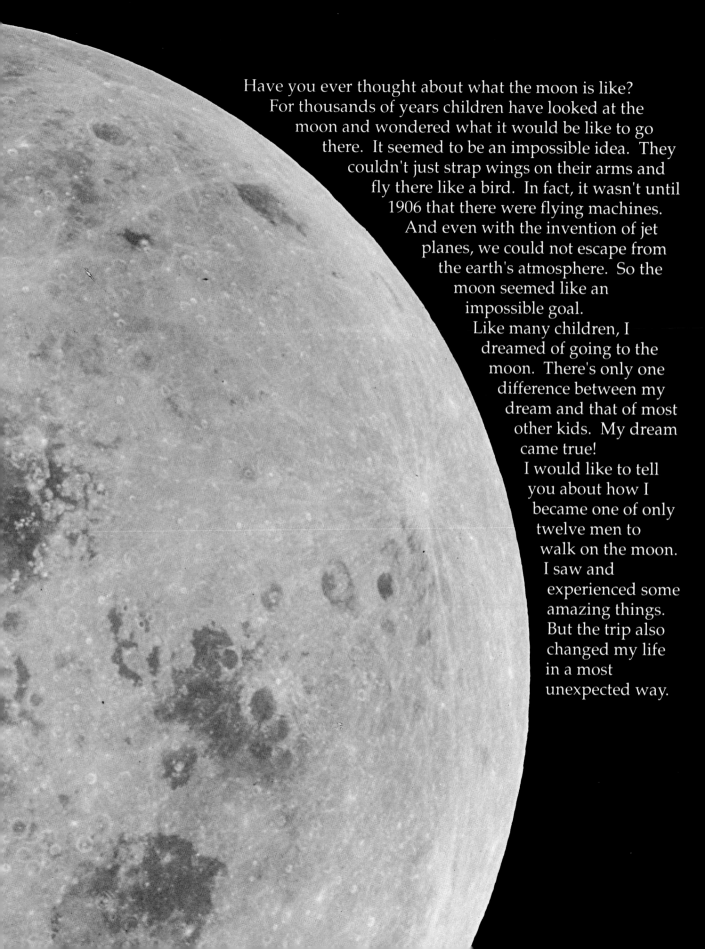

Have you ever thought about what the moon is like?
For thousands of years children have looked at the
moon and wondered what it would be like to go
there. It seemed to be an impossible idea. They
couldn't just strap wings on their arms and
fly there like a bird. In fact, it wasn't until
1906 that there were flying machines.
And even with the invention of jet
planes, we could not escape from
the earth's atmosphere. So the
moon seemed like an
impossible goal.
Like many children, I
dreamed of going to the
moon. There's only one
difference between my
dream and that of most
other kids. My dream
came true!
I would like to tell
you about how I
became one of only
twelve men to
walk on the moon.
I saw and
experienced some
amazing things.
But the trip also
changed my life
in a most
unexpected way.

Until 1957, space travel was only a fantasy. We could read stories about what it might be like. But that was only our imagination. Then the Soviet Union launched a satellite called Sputnik that circled the earth many times every day. Four years later, Yuri Gagarin became the first human being to fly in space.

The first American to orbit the earth was John Glenn. He was part of a program called Project Mercury. That was the first step towards the dream of President John F. Kennedy who challenged the United States to *commit itself to achieving the goal, before this decade is out, of landing a man on the moon and returning him safely to the earth.*

Each trip into space was a little longer and more complicated. After Project Mercury came Gemini where two men flew together. During some of these flights, an astronaut actually left his spacecraft and floated in space.

More astronauts were added to the space program as the time for moon flights drew closer. My, how I wanted to be one of those astronauts. But there was a problem. I was teaching a student how to fly and he lost control of the plane and we crashed into the desert. I was a mess--two broken legs, a broken jaw, and a banged-up head. It was so bad that the doctors wondered if I'd ever walk again. Fortunately, the student pilot also survived, though he had serious head injuries.

God was good to me and I did fly again. However, twice I applied for the space program and was turned down. They didn't tell me why, but it probably was because of my injuries from the plane crash. I was almost thirty-six years old, the point when I would be too old to be considered as an astronaut.

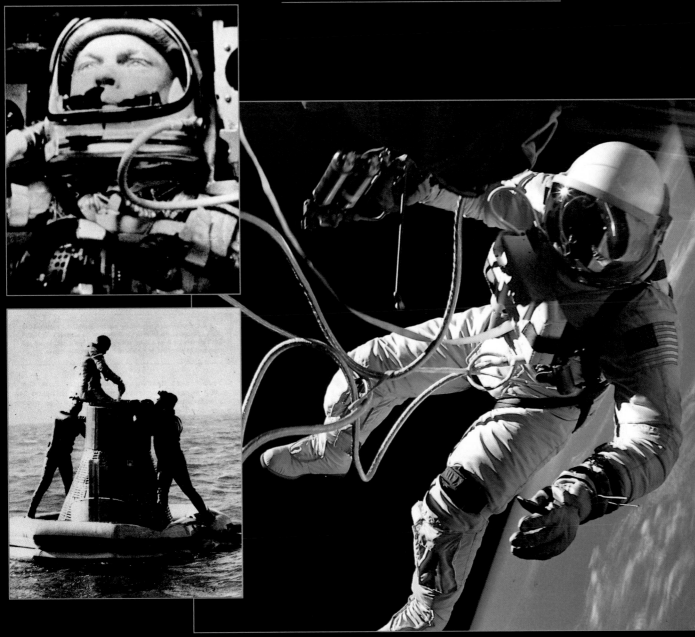

(Facing page, shown immediately prior to his historic flight on Vostok 1) *Cosmonanut Yuri Gagarin was the first human to fly into space. Americans Alan Shepard (bottom left) and Virgil Grissom (launch, facing page) had brief trips into space that lasted only a few minutes. Then on February 20, 1962 John Glenn (top and middle) orbited earth three times on a mission that gave America's space program much-needed momentum. For the next few years, NASA had an impressive stretch of successes, including Ed White's space walk in 1965 (below).*

There are so many things you have to learn if you want to be an astronaut. Sitting in school is not always fun. When I was bored, it helped to remember that I needed to learn these lessons if I wanted a chance to go into space.

Besides going to college, I had to learn how to fly airplanes. Then I went to a special school for test pilots, and another school for future astronauts. I learned about computers and how various rockets work. There were math and science classes. One course was called Orbital Mechanics. We learned how rockets launch satellites into space so they will stay there, orbiting the earth.

Before I became an astronaut, I worked on a top secret airplane called the YF12A. This plane set speed and altitude records for the United States. But for several years, I couldn't tell anyone about this exciting work, not even my family. I'm very proud of what I did on this plane and how my work helped my country.

However, my big dream was the moon. Because of my experience, I was allowed to apply a third time for the space program. I had to take a lot of special tests, including a very complete physical examination. I guess they wanted to make sure my head wasn't too scrambled from the plane crash. It must have been all right because this time I was accepted! And just in time; another few months and I would have reached the age limit.

Jim Irwin (fifth from left, second row) *was one of nineteen* **astronauts selected by NASA in April, 1966. Prior to this, Jim worked on the top secret YF12A plane** (below).

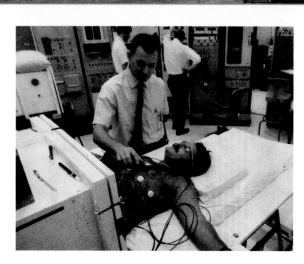

Centrifuge training allowed astronauts to experience the physical sensations of launch and reentry. After each ride in the centrifuge, they were tested to see how their bodies responded to those pressures. Basic training classes included jungle survival school (facing page) and geological field trips to places like Iceland.

I thought I'd learned a lot before I was an astronaut. But there were five more years of training ahead before my trip into space. Sometimes I thought my brain was going to explode because of all the information I had to remember. There were classes in subjects like astronomy (study of the stars), geology (study of rocks), and spacecraft design.

Fortunately, not all of our time was spent in classroom. We took field trips to factories that made the rockets and spacecrafts. We traveled around the world in order to understand the geology of earth compared to what we would see on the moon. We visited planetariums and observatories to practice our identification of stars.

Athletic training was important, too. We had to stay in top shape for the physical demands of space flight. We also spent time in a centrifuge. A centrifuge is a machine that spins astronauts around in a circle very fast so that we feel the pressures we will experience during launch and return to earth. Ever had an elephant sit on you? Well, that's how it feels when the centrifuge is going full speed.

Of course, once we're in space, we are weightless. If we aren't buckled into our seats, we float. It takes a while to get used to that. After all, I doubt that any of us have floated around our home or classroom, have we? That's because we are held on the earth by gravity.

There are two ways to learn how it feels to be weightless. One is by flying in an airplane many miles above the earth, then pushing the plane's nose down as if you were on a roller coaster starting down a steep incline. As you go over the top, you experience weightlessness for thirty to forty seconds. We'd do this hundreds of times. Sometimes all of that motion made me sick to my stomach. But usually it was fun floating around the airplane cabin.

Astronauts also learn how to scuba dive because you can experience the sensations of weightlessness under water. Also, by adding a little weight you can feel what it's like at one-sixth of earth's gravity, which is what we would experience on the moon.

We went to another school to learn how to fly helicopters. What do helicopters have to do with space flight? The lunar module that landed on the moon is actually a hovercraft that operates much like a helicopter.

As you can see, there was so much to do and learn that we had little time to relax. Sometimes we got very tired and missed being with our families.

Every aspect of space travel must be practiced. New astronauts learn the "feel" of weightlessness during zero-gravity training on an Air Force KC-135 airplane (left). An Apollo astronaut is lifted aboard a Coast Guard helicopter during a simulated recovery operation in the Gulf of Mexico (below). A Gemini pilot practices for a space walk in underwater zero-gravity training (facing page).

After our basic training was finished, we were assigned important jobs to do. My job was to test the lunar module that would land on the moon. Many changes were made on the entire Apollo system after a tragic fire killed three astronauts. We had to know if the changes would prevent another tragedy.

I took this job very seriously. You would, too, if you knew your life depended on your work. When you're on the moon, 250,000 miles away from home, no one can rescue you if something goes wrong. Since the moon doesn't have air, water, or food, we wouldn't live very long if, for some reason, we couldn't lift off. So you want to be sure that everything will work, even under the most difficult conditions.

Testing for the lunar module was done in a thermal vacuum chamber. This is a huge room where the air is pumped out to create a vacuum. Then the room is heated to more than 250 degrees Fahrenheit, which is the temperature on the surface of the moon when it's in the sunlight. You couldn't go into this room without wearing a space suit.

It took a year to run all of the tests. Only then could the contractors build the rest of the modules needed for the lunar flights. Of all the things I did as an astronaut, I think I'm proudest of this project because it was so difficult and also so important to the space program.

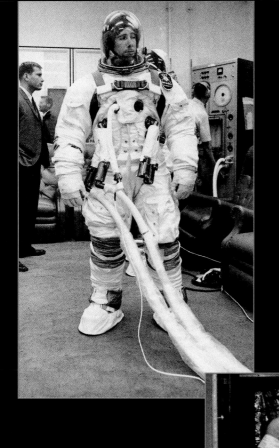

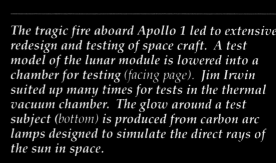

The tragic fire aboard Apollo 1 led to extensive redesign and testing of space craft. A test model of the lunar module is lowered into a chamber for testing (facing page). Jim Irwin suited up many times for tests in the thermal vacuum chamber. The glow around a test subject (bottom) is produced from carbon arc lamps designed to simulate the direct rays of the sun in space.

It was 1969, the year we had planned to land on the moon. The Apollo 10 mission was to be the final dress rehearsal. It would fly to the moon, and the lunar module would leave the command module and fly down to within fifty thousand feet of the surface.

My job was to support the crew of Apollo 10. The support team is a vital part of a mission. While the primary and backup crews train for the flight, the support team acts as their eyes to make sure all of their equipment works right.

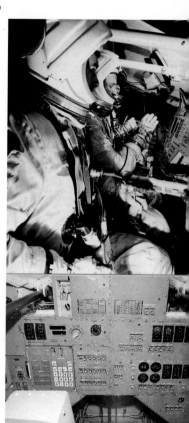

For me, this meant visiting many factories and carefully looking over the command module, service module, and lunar module. We ran many tests to make sure everything worked. The equipment didn't leave the factory until we said it was ready.

Then we watched as all of the parts of the rocket and spacecraft were put together in the Vehicle Assembly Building. That's one of the world's biggest buildings and it's just three miles from the launch pad. We made sure everything was connected and worked properly. Then the rocket was moved to the launch pad. There, we checked it out again before the primary crew took over.

The many parts of a rocket and space craft are assembled in the gigantic Vehicle Assembly Building (facing page). The 363-foot tall Apollo vehicle is then moved to the launch pad by a huge crawler-transporter. The primary, backup and support teams spend a lot of time inside the command module, testing the systems and training for launch day.

We apparently did our job well and the mission was a huge success. That paved the way for Apollo 11 and the historic moment two months later when Neil Armstrong became the first person to walk on the moon. I still get excited when I remember watching on television as Neil's foot touched lunar soil for the first time and he uttered the famous words, "That's one small step for man, one giant leap for mankind." I knew I had played an important role in helping to make this historical moment.

Now I wanted to take my turn to go to the moon. But I would have to wait a little longer.

I took a step closer when I was backup for Apollo 12, the second lunar landing. The backup crew trains for a mission the same way as the primary crew. If anything should happen to one of the primary crew members, the backup person is ready to step in and take over. Though I was ready, I wasn't needed for this flight.

There are many things that can go wrong in space. If we weren't so well prepared, we could easily become very afraid. The purpose of testing and training is to prevent as many mistakes and accidents as possible. But space travel is dangerous, and we all know that even with all of the preparation there are risks.

During Apollo 13, which was supposed to be the third landing on the moon, an oxygen tank exploded and severely damaged the service module. Oxygen, electricity, and water were lost to the command module. The three astronauts had to use the smaller lunar module as a lifeboat. Naturally, they couldn't land on the moon, and they had a very dangerous trip home.

Fortunately, a lot of people back on earth were ready to help. Several astronauts did experiments in simulators to find out what our friends needed to do to get home safely. Then Houston Control relayed instructions to the men in space. There was a sense of teamwork as we raced the clock to try and solve some huge problems. We felt like a sports team that through hard work defeats an unbeaten opponent against all odds. When the Apollo 13 crew returned safely, it felt like we'd won an Olympic championship!

The explosion of an oxygen tank on Apollo 13's service module made for a very dangerous journey home. One problem was a buildup of poisonous carbon dioxide gas. Technicians on the ground designed and tested a "mailbox" that filtered out the gas from the lunar module (facing page, insets). Astronauts also tested various maneuvers in a simulator (left). The damaged service module and lunar module were jettisoned in space just before Earth reentry.

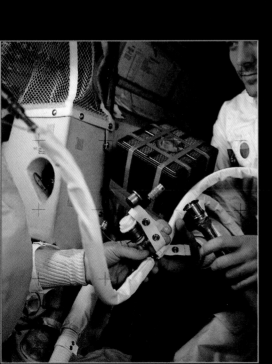
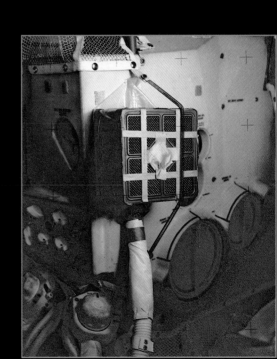

I got some great news in late 1969. I was selected to fly to the moon as part of the Apollo 15 crew. This is what I'd dreamed of for nearly forty years! Dave Scott was our mission commander, and he and I would descend to the moon. Al Worden would fly the command module and circle the moon for nearly three days while we went down for a look.

We thought we'd trained hard until now. But there was a lot more to learn. For one thing, we had to take an advanced course in lunar geology. This meant more field trips to places like Alaska, Mexico, Colorado, and Hawaii (that was my favorite!). Because we were going to land in the mountains of the moon, we particularly studied volcanoes, for we thought we might find evidence of volcanic activity on the moon.

Each field trip we practiced the procedures we'd use on the moon. Dave would choose a rock and set a pointer, called a gnoman, by it. Together we'd try to identify the kind of rock it was and I'd take several pictures of it. Only then did we pick

Training for the Apollo 15 mission included (left to right across the bottom): collecting a core sample; water egress training; desert survival training; pulling an equipment transporter; simulating exploration at one-sixth gravity; and using a lunar drill.

up the rock and place it in a numbered bag. In
this way we learned how to gather as much
scientific information as possible in the short time
we would have on the lunar surface.

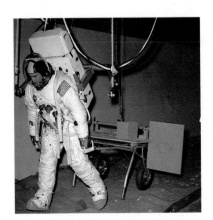

On this mission there was a new piece of equipment to help us explore more of the moon.

We would be the first astronauts to drive a car on another planet. We called it Rover and we practiced driving it a lot. That was fun, but we had to be careful. After all, it cost $8 million to build and test! We even got a special driver's license and license plate from General Motors.

Many of our practice sessions were done in the space suits. The lunar suits weigh sixty pounds on earth. Add to that a backpack that

weighs eighty pounds and you can see why it wasn't easy moving around. However, we knew they would be much lighter on the moon--only about twenty-three pounds for the suit and backpack.

We also spent hundreds of hours in simulators. This was how we practiced flying in space. All of the things we would see could be recreated in the simulator. For instance, photos and maps of the lunar surface were used to make very realistic models. We had everything except the dust. A camera moved over the surface as we worked the controls of the lunar module, practicing landings. We saw these pictures through our windows, so it was easy to imagine what it would be like for the real trip. We also could drive Rover using the simulator.

As we continued to practice, emergencies were put in to test our

Simulators allowed astronauts to practice every part of their space flights. Jim Irwin and Dave Scott spent a lot of time with the Lunar Roving Vehicle, both indoors and at various outdoor locations. Training time was also spent in the command module (below) and lunar module (below right).

skills and reactions. We'd be landing on the moon and one or more warning lights would flash. We'd have to decide whether or not to abort the landing and return to the command module. It was a little like playing a difficult video game, only much more serious. We knew that when we were on the trip for real, no one could rescue us if we got into trouble.

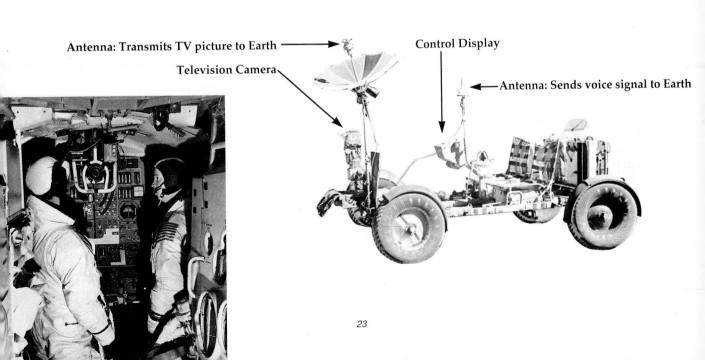

Antenna: Transmits TV picture to Earth

Television Camera

Control Display

Antenna: Sends voice signal to Earth

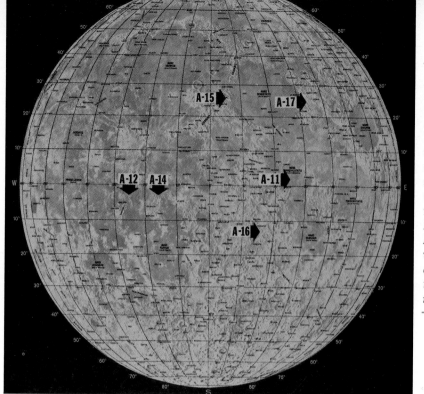

On each trip to the moon, a different landing site had been selected. Though the moon is one-fourth the size of earth, there was so much to explore that it was decided to visit as many different kinds of places as possible.

We might compare it to an explorer coming to earth from another planet. If that space traveler could only make five or six visits, he might go once to a mountain range, another time to a river valley, another to an ocean beach. He might make one stop in North America, another in Europe, a third in Asia. We took that same approach in our exploration of the moon.

The three landings before our flight had been in the lower, flatter areas that appear darker when we look at the moon. On our trip, it was decided to explore a mountainous area. I was thrilled with this decision because it meant we would see many new kinds of geological formations.

The choice was a site called Hadley Rille. A rille is like a canyon on earth. This one was more than one thousand feet deep and three thousand feet across. We would explore the rille, several craters, and a thirteen-thousand-foot mountain.

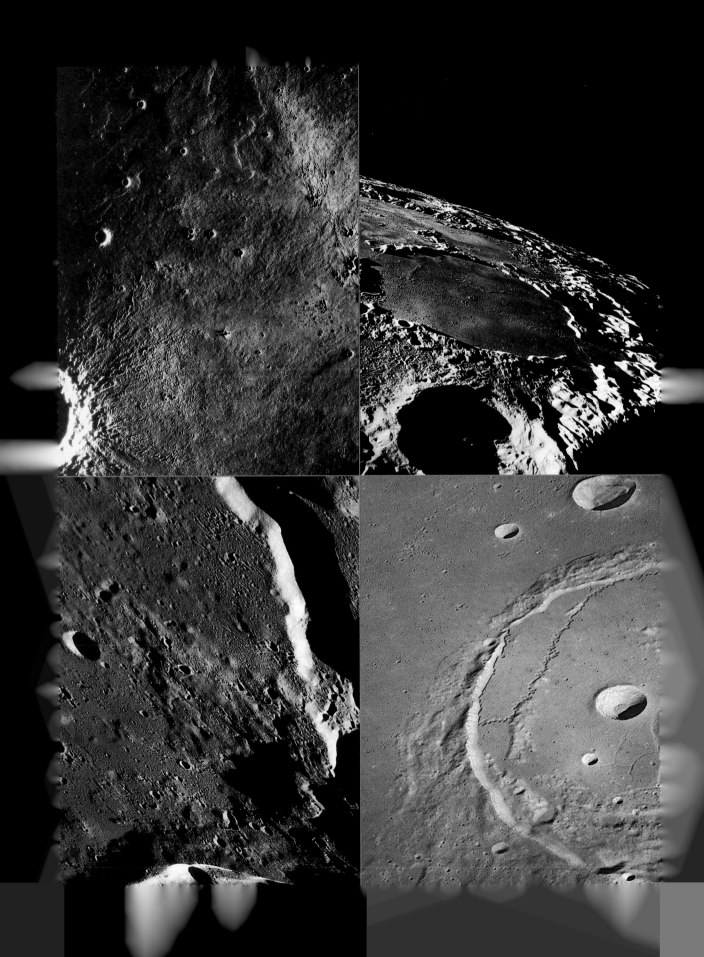

Finally, the big day arrived. It was still dark when we were awakened at 4:30 in the morning. "Okay, guys, are you ready to go to the moon?" said Deke Slayton, our boss. You bet we were ready!

First, a doctor gave us a brief physical examination. He wanted to be sure that we were completely healthy for the trip. Fortunately, all of us checked out fine. We certainly didn't want to miss this adventure because of a cold.

Then we had breakfast--steak, scrambled eggs, and orange juice. I really enjoyed that, knowing it was the last solid meal I'd have for nearly two weeks. Surprisingly, we were all quiet. We were each thinking about what was going to happen. No one wanted to disturb another's thoughts.

After breakfast it was time to put on our space suits. First, sensors were attached to our chests to monitor our heart rates and physical status. Then we put on long underwear and the suit. Finally our helmets were placed over our heads and we began breathing pure oxygen.

The air we normally breathe is only about one-fifth oxygen. Nitrogen and other gases make up the rest of our air. We had to breathe pure oxygen for three hours to get rid of the nitrogen in our bloodstream. Otherwise, it could produce dangerous bubbles in our blood, like the "bends" that scuba divers get. During this time, I tried to get a little more sleep.

Finally the call came to head for the launch pad. We had to carry a portable ventilator in one hand in order to keep breathing oxygen. Because I was the shortest, I had to hold my hose high so it didn't drag on the ground. I certainly didn't want a dirty hose!

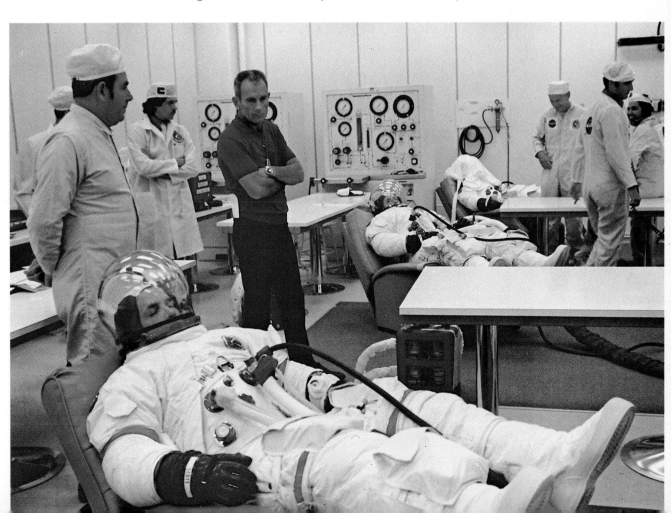

We rode an elevator up to our spacecraft, which we'd named *Endeavour*. Our seats were 360 feet off the ground. That's like going up thirty-six floors in a tall building. A crew helped us get into our couches, connect our hoses, and tighten the straps on our seat belts and shoulder harnesses. They checked electrical connections so we could talk to launch control at the Cape and to mission control in Houston.

Finally the door was shut. It made a big clang, like the sound of a dungeon door in a movie. That's when we knew this was for real. The waiting was over; we were going to the moon!

We heard the last seconds of countdown: "Ten, nine, eight . . . three, two, one, ignition!

"You have liftoff."

I still can recall all of the sensations and emotions of my trip. It's as if I am reliving it again today. When we hear "ignition" at the end of the countdown, we don't feel much. There is a muffled roar and just a slight vibration. Then, quickly, the pressure on us begins to build. Fortunately, there is little to do. So far everything is proceeding smoothly.

This is almost the happiest moment of my life. There are tears coming down my face. All the tensions leading up to this flight are gone. I want to enjoy every sensation.

Looking out the window I see the blue sky getting blacker and blacker as we leave earth's atmosphere. Within twelve minutes we are in orbit more than one hundred miles above the earth, traveling over seventeen thousand miles an hour. At that speed, we go around the earth in just ninety minutes. On one side of the spacecraft, we see the blue oceans of earth. On the other, the blackness of space.

But there isn't much time to enjoy the view. We have a lot of work to do, checking out all of the systems before we head for the moon. Then

Third Stage
Second Stage
First Stage

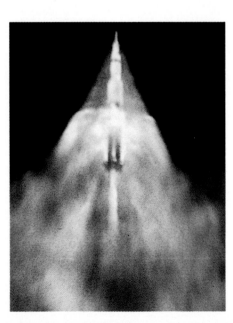

Ignition of the second stage of the Saturn V rocket and separation of the first stage rocket occurred 38 miles above earth, two minutes and forty seconds after launch (below, facing page). The third stage shoved the Apollo spacecraft towards the moon, giving the three astronauts a spectacular view of the Hawaiian Islands (below).

there is another countdown and ignition of the third stage of the Saturn rocket. This is the TLI or Translunar Injection burn that allows us to break away from the gravitational pull of earth and head towards the moon.

For five minutes we feel like we're riding a powerful elevator. I look out my window and see all of the Hawaiian Islands. When the rocket shuts down, we are traveling twenty-five thousand miles an hour, but there is no sensation of speed. When you ride in a car, you know you are moving because you see things going by outside the window. But in space, there are no trees or ground going by, and the earth, moon, and stars are so far away that you don't see them move. So, though we're traveling faster than man has ever gone before, it doesn't feel like we're moving at all.

It takes us three days to fly to the moon. During this time we have many duties, but there is also time to look back at the earth. It reminds me of a Christmas tree ornament hanging in the blackness of space. It looks so fragile, as if it would crumble if I reached out and touched it. By the time we arrive at the moon, Earth is the size of a marble--the prettiest marble I've ever seen.

We fire an engine to slow us down so we don't fly past our destination. When we turn the rocket off, we're in an orbit around the moon. What a sight it is when we suddenly see the moon's surface for the first time. It doesn't look real. Its dark gray color makes it look like a huge lump of clay.

After orbiting the moon for a day, Dave and I put on our suits and transfer into the lunar module, which we've called *Falcon*. We find that the glass covering of the landing radar display has shattered and pieces of glass are floating around the cabin. We carefully grab the large pieces with sticky tape and hope the rest will be collected in a screen as we turn on the circulation fan.

We are eager to go down to the surface, but at first *Falcon* won't undock. It's stuck! Al has to check all of the connections, then we try again. This time it works. We move away from *Endeavour* and our orbit drops until it looks like we will crash

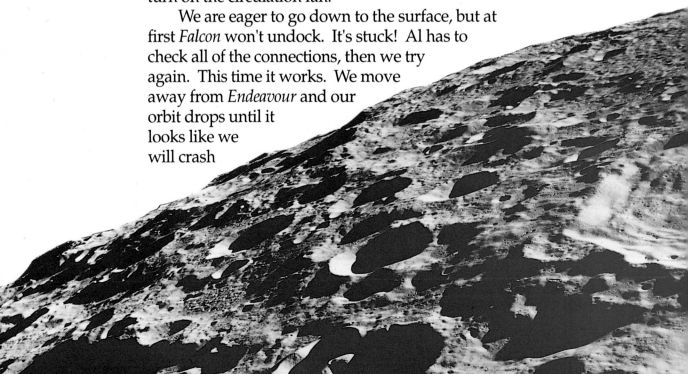

into some of the high mountains on the moon. But that's just an illusion. The computer has everything programmed, so we aren't in any danger.

We start the descent rocket and begin a twelve-minute landing procedure. Soon Mount Hadley is towering above us. But I can't sightsee yet because I am concentrating on our computer and other instruments, relaying information to Dave who is flying the machine.

About one hundred feet from the surface, dust begins to stir from the exhaust of our engines. There is a probe at the bottom of the landing gear, and when it touches the surface a light comes on. "Contact!" I announce, and Dave immediately shuts down the engine. We fall the final few feet and land very hard. "BAM!" I exclaim.

For a moment we start tilting to one side. Should we abort and take off immediately? We freeze until the *Falcon* stops moving. We have landed on the rim of a small crater. But we are safe! We hold our breath for a few more moments until mission control says we're cleared to stay.

The Apollo missions provided spectacular, never-before-seen views of earth. The above photo (top, left) shows the south polar ice cap and much of Africa and the Asian mainland. Mt. Hadley towered over Falcon as it landed. Lunar distances are deceiving. Though Hadley looks close, it is actually 20 miles away.

Dave and I help each other put on our space suits. Then we depressurize the cabin before Dave opens the door and goes down the ladder. As his foot touches the surface of the moon, he announces, "Man must explore. And this is exploration at its greatest!"

I'm next, but I get stuck in the door. I finally wiggle free and start down the ladder. When my foot touches the lunar surface, I lose my balance and start to fall. All I can think about is that millions of people around the world are watching me in this most embarrassing moment! I manage to keep one hand on the ladder and fall to the side, out of the camera's view.

As we look around, I can only compare what I see to a desert, but without cactus or any other signs of life. The powdery dust we walk on is three inches deep. On earth, I weigh 156 pounds, but on the moon I only weigh 26 pounds. So I am able to travel farther with each step I take. Dave looks a little like a kangaroo bounding as he walks. I feel like I am walking on a trampoline.

Hadley Rille is a winding canyon 1,100 feet deep and 3,000 feet across (above). The astronauts wanted to explore it but it was too dangerous to drive down. One of Jim Irwin's assignments was to make a trench in the lunar soil (top, right).

We unpack Rover and start driving towards Hadley Rille, which is about a mile away. Though we can only go about ten miles per hour at best, it seems like we are moving faster. The ride feels a little like riding a bucking bronco. Because of the low gravity, every time we hit a bump, we float for a moment before hitting the ground again. I'm glad we have our seatbelts fastened.

At the rille, Dave suggests we drive down into it for a close look. "You go ahead," I say. "I'll wait right here." Actually, Houston won't let us go down. If we got stuck, we wouldn't have enough oxygen to climb back out of the canyon.

After picking up some rock samples, we drive back to the landing site to set up some important experiments. One will measure the heat flowing from the core of the moon. Another will collect high energy particles from the sun. A third will chart any seismic activity from moonquakes or meteors hitting the lunar surface. There's also a mirror to reflect a laser beam from earth, allowing scientists to accurately measure the distance between earth and the moon.

I have to pull some strings and release several bolts and pins in order to erect the transmitter for the experiments. I am almost done when a string breaks and I can't reach the last pin. This failure never happened in practice. Time is running out and I don't know what to do. Immediately I pray, "God, what shall I do?"

I seem to hear, "Jim, down on your knees!" I get down on my knees and see I can release the final pin without pulling the string. The station pops right up.

Our first lunar exploration lasts six-and-a-half hours. Before going back into the module to eat and rest, we dust each other off with a brush. Each of us has fallen a couple of times, so we're covered with a layer of fine black dust. When we remove our suits in the *Falcon* cabin, Dave and I immediately notice a strong smell like that of gunpowder. Apparently we didn't brush off all of the lunar dust, and when it's exposed to oxygen for the first time it gives off that strong odor.

When we awaken from our sleep we discover a water leak. With directions from mission control, we fix the leak and dump the extra water into special containers. It's fortunate that our module landed at a slight angle on the rim of a crater. If it had tilted the other way, the water would have flowed into a mass of electrical equipment. That could have shorted connections, perhaps leaving us unable to lift off. We would have been stranded on the moon.

Our destination today is the base of Mount

Hadley Delta. Our purpose is to find rocks that might help us understand the origin of lunar mountains. We park by Spur Crater and discover rocks of light green and brown. But one in particular catches our attention. We've been asked to find a white rock, and there it is. It sits on a pedestal looking like a museum display.

When we get back to earth, we learn that this is the oldest rock ever discovered. The news media named it the Genesis Rock.

Many people consider the phototograph of Astronaut James Irwin (facing page) the most famous lunar photo ever taken. The most important discovery of Apollo 15 was the white rock sitting on top of its natural pedestal (left). The instument next to the rock is called a gnoman. The layering in the mountains (above left and right) surprised the astronauts and seemed to suggest that the moon's surface was built up in stages.

After a little extra sleep, we are ready for our third and final outing on the moon. The first assignment is to try and get a core sample using a lunar drill. This ten-foot-long rock sample will allow scientists to better understand what it is like under the lunar surface. But the drill gets stuck. It takes both of us heaving with all our strength to remove that core sample.

Though it is still early morning on the moon, we are beginning to feel the heat. We can't stay much longer. During our drive, Dave remarks, "Look at the mountains. When they're all sunlit, isn't that beautiful?"

I answer, "Dave, I'm reminded of my favorite biblical passage from the psalms: 'I will lift up mine eyes unto the hills. From whence cometh my help?' Of course, we get quite a bit of help from Houston." I know I am also getting help from another Source.

Back at the base, Dave does "The Galileo Experiment" in honor of the famous scientist who

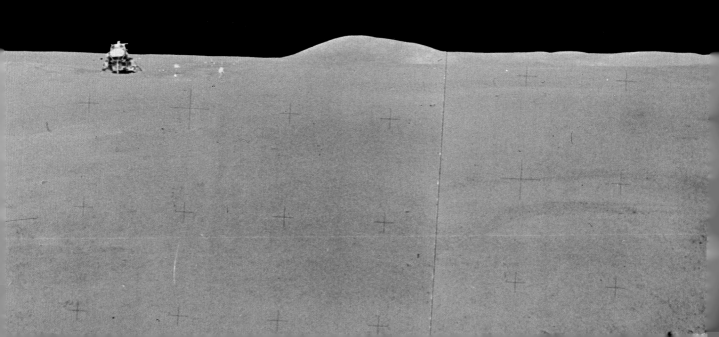

discovered the principles of gravity. Galileo believed that without any air, all objects, regardless of size and weight, would fall at the same speed. So Dave holds up a hammer and a feather and drops them at the same time. Sure enough, in airless environment the hammer and feather float-fall at the same rate and hit the ground 1.3 seconds later.

Now it's time to start packing for the trip home. But first I have a few unplanned minutes. I run around the lunar module and do some broad jumps—in short, act like a kid. Boy, that's fun!

Then I stop and think about where I am. I'm in awe of what man has accomplished through technology. But something else is happening in me. As I look around at God's creation I have an overwhelming sense of His Presence. I feel God is calling me to Himself, and that He will give me a new mission when this one is completed.

Jim Irwin left a plaque (above) on the moon in memory of 14 NASA astronauts and USSR cosmonauts who had died. The tiny, man-like object represents the figure of a fallen astronaut/cosmonaut.

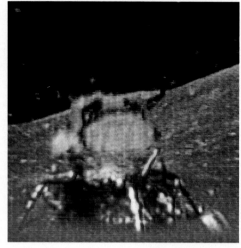

There is a lot of work to do before lift-off. We store the rocks and soil samples. The weight of the rocks means we must leave behind some items we don't need. We leave a big trash bag with the empty containers from our meals. Rover has to stay behind, too. I don't like the thought that our campsite is strewn with things we don't need.

We've also left some souvenirs, including a coin with the fingerprints of my four children. It's strange to realize that our footprints will be here for a million years. And the other items--perhaps for eternity. If you want a good used car, you know where to find one.

We're so busy that we almost miss lift-off. Fortunately, the computer doesn't forget. The ascent stage engine fires automatically, sounding like a whistling wind. One moment we are on the moon, the next we are a hundred feet above the surface. I take one last look and see the descent

FALCON

Lift-off from the moon was recorded by the TV camera on Rover (facing page, top). A few minutes later, Astronauts Irwin and Scott spotted the command and service modules (right). The service module contained sophisticated cameras that photographed much of the lunar surface, such as the view below showing the line between lunar night and day. Hadley Rille (facing page, lower right) was photographed from lunar orbit after Falcon rejoined Endeavour.

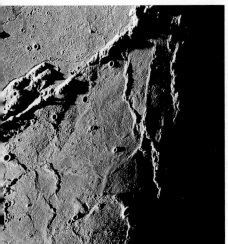

stage, Rover, the scientific base, and all the tracks we've made.

It takes only seven minutes before we shut down the engine and are in orbit around the moon. Now we have to find the command module. Meanwhile, we are weightless again, and all the lunar dust starts floating. I'm glad we have our helmets on so it doesn't get into our eyes.

Carefully we approach *Endeavour*. There is a dull thud as the two modules dock. Al opens his hatch and says, "Welcome home!"

Of course, we are still 250,000 miles from earth. We transfer the valuable lunar samples into the command module, then jettison *Falcon*. It's kind of sad to know that our faithful lunar module will crash into the moon. But we can't afford to carry it back with us.

For the first time in the trip, I feel very tired. Mission control tells us all to get some much-needed sleep.

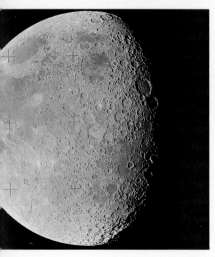

We spend two more days in lunar orbit before heading back to earth. This allows us to take some special photographs. Many of these photographs will help NASA decide the site of future lunar landings.

When we are on the sunny side of the moon, it is uncomfortably hot, even in our underwear. On the dark side, it cools down to a comfortable temperature. About the time we are getting comfortable, we come back to the sunlit side.

One of the most critical moments of the entire trip is what is called the Trans-Earth Injection Burn. This occurs behind the moon where we are unable to communicate with Houston. The rocket must fire at exactly the right moment to release us from the moon's gravity and shove us back towards earth. We also have to be directed at just the right angle so we don't skip off the earth's atmosphere back into space or burn up like a shooting star. Fortunately, our equipment is very reliable, and the burn goes perfectly.

The highlight of our trip home is Al's walk in space. He has to retrieve the film used in cameras on the service module, which we jettison before entering earth's atmosphere. When we open the hatch, it's like a vacuum cleaner sucking out everything that's loose. My toothbrush and a camera start floating out into space. Fortunately, I am able to grab them, but I do lose a comb.

I lean out of the spacecraft as Al takes his walk in space. What a sight! I'm looking out into absolute blackness. Because there is so much

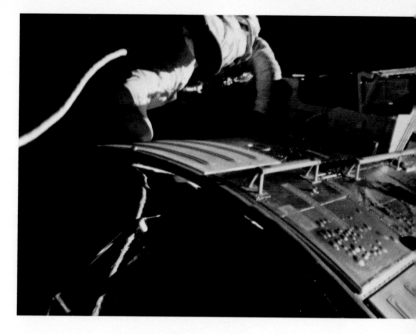

Approximately 171,000 miles from Earth, Al Worden stepped out of his spacecraft to retrieve film cassettes from the panoramic and mapping cameras in the service module.

light from the sun, I can't see any stars and the earth is only a thin crescent. It's an eerie experience; I feel like an alien.

For Al, this is the highlight of his trip. He describes how directly behind me is a brilliant full moon. He wants to stay out and enjoy the beautiful sight. I can't wait to get back into the security of our spacecraft.

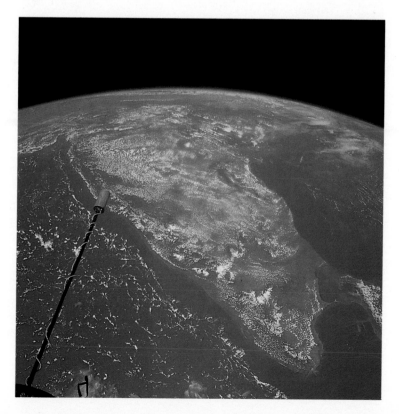

The biggest shock when we return to earth is going from weightlessness to 8G's (eight times earth gravity) during reentry. For about four minutes it is impossible to lift an arm. Even breathing is difficult.

At fifty thousand feet above the ocean, a drogue parachute comes out to slow our descent. At ten thousand feet, three large chutes open. Except one of the chutes fails, so we're falling faster than expected. For a moment I'm afraid we might have a tragic end to our trip.

We hit the water hard, and instantly I hit a switch releasing the chutes so they won't pull *Endeavour* over.

We go under water for a moment, then pop back up like a giant cork. We're back on earth!

Navy frogmen quickly surround the module and wave to us through the window. When they open the hatch, we pile out into a life raft. A helicopter lowers a net which lifts each of us up. A few minutes later, we're on an aircraft carrier greeting NASA officials, congressmen, generals, and admirals.

At first it is a little hard to walk because we've been in space for twelve days, experiencing weightlessness for most of the time. However, it sure feels great to be home! And we don't have to go into quarantine. For the first three Apollo missions, the crew spent three weeks in isolation to make sure they were not carrying any unknown germs back to earth. But scientists have decided that it is safe to touch us.

Our work isn't finished yet. We have several weeks of debriefing, where we tell scientists and NASA officials everything we learned on our trip. We also need time to recover physically and be reunited with our families. Then we visit our President and take a trip around the world, telling people about what we saw on the moon.

Apollo 15's return to earth had a little extra excitement when one of the parachutes failed to open. However, the astronauts arrived home safely to a warm reunion with family and friends. Meanwhile, analysis began on the 170 pounds of lunar rock and soil samples from the mission. Each sample was weighed, measured, and classified before going to scientists around the world for study.

Ever since the historic mission of Apollo 15, I've been telling people about my trip. That includes my spiritual experience, for what happened to me on the moon changed my life forever. Before the trip, I was so absorbed with preparations that I never thought how high the spiritual flight could be. Now I believe God wanted me to go to the moon so I could come back and do something more important with my life than fly airplanes or a spacecraft. That's why I now travel anywhere in the world that people will have me--to tell them about my trip and also about my relationship with God.

Many men and women have flown in space since my flight. There were two more trips to the moon. There was the Sky Lab project where astronauts worked for many months in space. There was a joint flight where an Apollo capsule linked up with a Soyez spacecraft from the Soviet Union. The Soviets have set up a space station where cosmonauts can work for a year at a time. And of course, there are the American and Soviet space shuttles

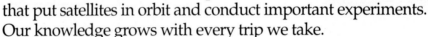

that put satellites in orbit and conduct important experiments. Our knowledge grows with every trip we take.

What is the future of space travel? One real possibility is a trip to Mars. There is talk that the Soviet Union and the United States might join together for this incredible journey. Who knows, perhaps you will be one of the crew members. Or perhaps you will journey to farther reaches of our solar system, to Jupiter or beyond.

A few years ago, such thoughts were impossible dreams. But they aren't anymore. In fact, they're far more possible than my crazy dream of going to the moon was when I was a boy. So don't be afraid to dream big dreams. Yes, shoot for the stars!

But I think its even more important to recognize the Creator of this great planet and the universe in which it exists. After all, He is the one who created the laws of science that make space travel possible. With God in control of our lives, not only can we explore other planets, we have hope for this planet. With His help, you and I can have a part in making earth a better place for all of us.

Seventeen years after the flight of Apollo 15, James Irwin made a special presentation to General Secretary Mikhail Gorbachev of the Soviet Union. Jim took the Soviet flag with him as a small token of the tremendous achievements of the Soviet space program.

Photo Credits:

All photos provided courtesy of the National Aeronautics and Space Administration unless otherwise noted.

Page 6: *(left)* TASS from Sovfoto; *(right)* Mercury 4. **Page 7:** *(top and middle)* John Glenn, Mercury 6; *(bottom left)* Alan Shepard, Mercury 3; *(bottom right)* Gemini 4. **Pages 8, 9:** YF12A courtesy of Department of Defense Still Media Records. **Page 8:** Portrait of Irwin, July 1971. **Page 9:** Astronauts Class of 1966. **Pages 10, 11:** Centrifuge photos from Manned Spacecraft Center, Houston, Texas. Jungle training class, June 1967, and Geology training, July 1967. **Page 12:** Zero gravity training, February 1967; Apollo 15 Water Egress training. **Page 13:** Gemini 12 underwater training. **Page 14:** *(top)* Apollo 1 fire; *(bottom)* LTA-8 testing. **Page 15:** *(top)* Jim Irwin, LTA-8; *(middle)* James Irwin, foreground, and Grumman Aircraft Engineering pilot, LTA-8; *(bottom)* Test subject Robert Piljay prior to start of LTA-8 tests. **Page 16:** *(top and bottom, left)* Apollo 10 Assembly; *(right)* Apollo 15 being moved to launch pad. **Page 17:** *(top)* Apollo Critical Design Review activity, February 1966; *(bottom)* Apollo Command Module controls, April 1966. **Page 18:** Apollo Training Facility, Manned Spacecraft Center, Houston, Texas; **Page 19:** Apollo 13. **Page 20:** *(left and middle)* Apollo 15; *(right)* Desert survival training, August 1967. **Page 21:** *(left)* Equipment test, February 1970; *(middle)* Lunar simulation, April 1965; *(right)* Apollo 15; *(top)* Apollo 15 crew, March 1971. **Page 22:** Rover license provided courtesy of Ferenc Pavlics and General Motors; Rover practice, Apollo 15; *(bottom)* Command Module interior, May 1967, courtesy of North American Aviation, Inc. **Page 23:** *(top)* Apollo 15 EVA simulation; *(bottom)* Apollo 9 lunar module simulator training. **Page 24:** *(top)* Apollo landing sites; *(bottom)* Apollo 15. **Page 25:** Apollo 15. **Pages 26, 27:** Apollo 15. **Pages 28, 29:** Apollo 15. **Page 30:** *(bottom, right and left)* Apollo 11. **Pages 30, 31:** Apollo 15. **Page 31:** Space Shuttle, October 1988. **Page 32:** *(top)* Apollo 17; *(bottom)* Apollo 11. **Page 33:** Apollo 15. **Pages 34, 35:** Apollo 15. **Pages 36, 37:** Apollo 15. **Pages 38, 39:** Apollo 15. **Page 40:** *(top)* Apollo 17; *(bottom)* Apollo 15. **Page 41:** Apollo 15. **Pages 42, 43:** Apollo 15. **Page 44:** Apollo 15 lunar samples. **Page 45:** Apollo 15. **Page 46:** Apollo-Soyuz, July 1975. **Page 47:** *(top, left)* Space Shuttle *Challenger*, August 1983; *(bottom, left)* Space Shuttle *Challenger*, April 1984; *(top, right)* Viking Lander 2; *(middle)* Voyager 1; *(bottom, right)* Voyager 2. **Page 48:** Associated Press Photo.

A special thank you to Lisa Vasquez-Morrison, still photo researcher at NASA Lyndon B. Johnson Space Center.